HOW TO GET RID
OF A
TELEMARKETER

by Mrs. Millard America
and the editors of

BAD
DOG
PRESS™

Bad Dog Press
P.O. Box 130066
Roseville, MN 55113

e-mail: badogpress@aol.com & badogbook@aol.com

How to Get Rid of a Telemarketer

First published in 1996

Printed in the United States of America.
96 97 98 99 00   5 4 3 2 1

Text: Tony Dierckins and Tim Nyberg
Illustrations: Tim Nyberg

ISBN 1-887317-01-5
Library of Congress Catalog Card Number: 95-83149

Warning: Contains humor, a highly volatile substance if used improperly.
Harmful if swallowed. All content is a fictional product of the authors'
imaginations. Any resemblance between characters portrayed herein and
actual persons living, dead, or residing in New Jersey is purely coinciden-
tal. Contents under pressure. Do not use near open flame. Do not use as
a flotation device, or at least avoid any situations in which you would
need to rely on a book as a flotation device. Any typographic errors are
purely intentional and left for your amusement. Always say no to drugs
and, by all means, stay in school.

Bad Dog Press would like to thank
the following folks for helping us get things
off the ground:

Adventure Publications,
the Law Offices of Patrick D. Moren,
the late great Richard Drew
(father of strip adhesives),
and, of course, our own bad dogs,
Kirby, Danté, and James.

CONTENTS

Preface

Hello. My name is Mrs. Millard America. This is my first book. You may know me from my radio show, "Helpful Household Hints for Happy Homemakers." A few years back I did an episode about getting rid of telemarketers. The show received an overwhelming response and nominations for several prestigious honors, including the coveted "Happy Homemaker Award," which I awarded to myself.

It also won the attention of Bad Dog Press, and since then those nice folks have been buggin' the heck out of me to write a book about the topic.

Well, I'm not much of a writer. I'd rather spend my time pondering new ways to handle difficult household tasks or organizing my Spam® and Velveeta® recipes. But when I heard Paul Harvey say that telemarketers made about $250 billion in 1994, I figured I'd better write this book!

Don't get me wrong, I don't hate telemarketers. I'm sure most of them are really very nice people. It's just that I don't like them calling me at dinner time pretending like they know me—or breaking in on call waiting when I'm talking to my neighbor, Caroline. Or worse yet, selling

Millard $400 worth of ductwork cleaning when he knows darned well we have hot-water heat!

I think we all have a tremendous responsibility to help these poor dear souls get different types of jobs before they slip any further into the sleazy, inescapable chasm of permanent telemarketerdom (and before those of us who fall prey to their clever trickery lose our life savings).

If you can't hang up on telemarketers—and hate yourself for it—this book is for you.

If you are a telemarketer, this book may help you recognize the error of your ways and get you on the course to recovery so you can still live a full and meaningful life. If it helps you, don't feel obliged to call to express your gratitude—the silence of the phone will be thanks enough.

Have a good good day.

June

—Mrs. Millard (June) America

CHAPTER 1

BE PREPARED

The telephone should be an agent of joy. It bridges the miles between loved ones, saves lives through 911 service, and connects us to the pizza guy. Telemarketing, however, has turned the phone into an instrument of terror. We no longer jump to the phone each time it rings, anxious to discover who's reaching out to touch us. Instead we cringe in fear, wondering if a solicitor waits to pounce on us with another sales pitch.

Confronting telemarketers need not cause you stress. The key is preparation. In this chapter, you will learn quick and efficient identification of a sales call as well as some the disturbing details of many telemarketers' lives—new knowledge that will help free you from phone solicitors.

IDENTIFYING A TELEMARKETER

Each time the phone rings there is a chance that a tele-marketer looms on the other end of the line. To success-fully rid yourself of an annoying sales call, you must remain prepared to act immediately. Therefore, identifying a telemarketer as soon as—or better yet, before—you pick up the receiver is essential to implementing effective anti-telemarketer techniques. Follow the procedures outlined on the following pages to prepare yourself to handle unwanted calls.

▲ *Although this method is effective, there are better ways to avoid telemarketing calls.*

1. RECOGNIZE THE RING

Always consider the activity in which you are engaged when the telephone first rings. There is at least a fifty percent chance that you are about to have an encounter with a telemarketer if you are:

- Watching your favorite TV show.
- Taking a bath.
- Changing a diaper.
- Eating dinner.
- Engaged in "marital relations."
- Leaving the house, late for an engagement.
- Reading in the bathroom.
- Napping.
- Painting the ceiling.
- Burning cookies.

June Says: Oh, hello there! June here. Do you have that call waiting on your phone? If you're talking long-distance with an old friend and someone "beeps in," chances are a good 85% that the new caller wants to sell you something!

2. RECOGNIZE THE GREETING

To deflect a sales call effectively, you must be able to identify a telemarketer and hang up (or take charge of the call—your choice) before he or she can squeeze off seven words. If a caller answers your greeting in any of the following ways, you have a phone salesperson on the line:

- "Hello" (spoken in a sing-songy, way-too-chipper voice for the current time of day).

- "Is this the man of the house?"

- "Is this the woman of the house?"

- "Is this Mr. [your last name] ?"

- "Is this Miss [your last name] ?"

- "Is this Mrs. [your husband's last name—which you never took] ?"

- "Is this [your name phonetically mispronounced] ?"

- "Is this [your name as it appears in the phone book, but as no one you know would ever call you, except maybe your parents when, as a child, you did something wrong] ?"

June Says: Oh, hello there! June here. Are you wondering what to do if you think you have a sales call, but the caller answers in a way that doesn't immediately identify them as a telemarketer? Well, don't panic. Just say "Yes?" to however they greet you, then listen closely. If they respond, "And how are you this evening?" you've got a telemarketer on the line!

▲ *"Telephonus Interruptus"? Let the machine get it: odds are you've got a phone solicitor on the line!*

3. LISTEN BEFORE SAYING "HELLO"

If the timing of a call suggests that a telemarketer waits on the other end, don't greet the caller as you pick up the receiver. Instead, pause and listen carefully for the following clues:

- As telemarketers wait for your greeting, you can usually hear the background cacophony of their colleagues as they make similar intrusions into the lives of other unsuspecting souls. If so, hang up.

- If the telemarketing firm annoying you uses computers to make contact, their machine will begin "speaking" shortly after you pick up the phone. If you hear a prerecorded or computerized voice, treat this as a sign from above that you may hang up at any time.

- Many telemarketing firms attack nationwide. If you hear the not-so-clear "fuzz" of a long-distance call, get ready to hang up. If the caller speaks with an accent from a region of the country other than your own, it doesn't matter how they greet you: they're telemarketers. Disconnect them.

Know Your Adversary

OK, so now you know how to tell when you are about to encounter a telemarketer. But do you really know who you're dealing with? Most people are reluctant to simply hang up on telemarketers. They think, "Hey, this person's only trying to make a living," and end up wasting precious time conversing with a phone salesperson. We believe, however, that once you understand what telemarketers can become if they stay in the industry long enough, you'll want to do whatever you can to encourage them to find other work. Encouragement begins when you hang up.

To help you get to know your adversary, we've enlisted the help of Dr. Arvid Breckenbloom, a renowned sociologist famous for *The Chimpanzee and Call Waiting*, his breakthrough work in primate neurosis due to untimely interruption. Dr. Breckenbloom examined the résumé of "Bob Johnson" (not his real name) on page 8. "Bob" is a typical telemarketer living in a typical midwestern city. Compare Bob's résumé with Dr. Breckenbloom's accompanying interpretive observations.

Actual Résumé of a Telemarketer

Bob Johnson
502 North 12th Avenue East
Duluth, MN 55812

Education:

Technical degree in mobile home repair
received in June 1995 from Al and Sid's
University of the Lower East Side.

Previous Employment:

1993 - 1995. Assistant Manager, Pete's Pork
Emporium. Responsibilities: Supervising
employees, overseeing deep fryer safety,
official "trichinosis patroller."

1990 - 1993. Lawn Maintenance Engineer,
Bob's Lawn Care. Responsibilities: owned and
operated private lawn care service specializing
in grass height control and sidewalk edge
enhancement.

1986 - 1990. Circulation Associate, The
Duluth Dispatch. Responsibilities: Personally
ensuring the daily delivery of the company
product to over thirty individual clients within
a specific suburban region.

Hobbies/Special Interests:

Evaluating effectiveness of daytime talk show
guest panels; compiling videocassette collection
of the works of American celluloid artists
Hanna-Barbera.

DR. BRECKENBLOOM'S INTERPRETIVE ANALYSIS

Education: "If they, in fact, do have any postsecondary education, most telemarketers attended technical schools with questionable accreditation or hold legitimate B.A.s in some liberal or fine arts discipline. This background, of course, renders them as unemployable as most high school dropouts. But unlike high school dropouts, they have student loans to repay—and a minimum wage telemarketing job doesn't even begin to help pay the rent."

Previous Employment: "Telemarketers have taken jobs in phone sales because they have no real previous work experience, at least none that has provided them with any real job skills. Many gained some telecommunication skills using a phone headset while working at fast-food drive-through windows. Others may have cut lawns or had a paper route, but failed to parlay their skills into the landscaping or information distribution industries. Often, therefore, telemarketing is their first real job and last career choice."

Hobbies / Special Interests: "Telemarketers work odd hours, often in four-hour shifts, and usually in the early evening or weekends when they can find their victims at home trying to eat dinner and relax after eight hours of constructive labor. Consequently, ideal telemarketers seldom have outside interests that require free time during evenings and weekends. Usually they sit around and watch "Geraldo," "Ricki Lake," "Jenny Jones," and "Gilligan's Island" reruns.

Overview: "Without our intervention, typical telemarketers can become loathsome souls. Forced to work odd hours in a low-paying job that they would rather not have and to face the constant rejection of annoyed "potential customers," average telemarketers are emotional wrecks. They also don't date very often because they fear further rejection and their job schedules don't leave them free for traditional dating activities.

"After work, most telemarketers go straight to the local bar, where they drink, complain about work, and end up in destructive relationships with other telemarketers, themselves filled with similar personal disappointments. They wake each day around noon, hung over and too late to hit the pavement and find a better job. They eat a little something (usually macaroni and cheese), watch "The Flintstones," and take the bus to work, where the cycle begins again.

"Bitter and unfulfilled in their careers and personal lives (and facing mounting debts), many telemarketers become desperate little people who will stop at nothing to earn their commission.

"These observations, of course, are based on my personal speculation. A true evaluation would require years of research and millions of dollars in government grants."

June Says: **Oh, hello there! June here. Thanks, Doc! That was really enlightening! As you can see, readers, to face the enemy, you must be strong. You must not give in to their desperation, but rather take advantage of their vulnerability. Try to think of getting rid of a telemarketer as helping him or her: if we all constantly battle the onslaught of calls, we may force telemarketers out of work and, God willing, into better careers. Think of it this way: each time you hang up, you may very well be helping to save a life.**

CHAPTER 2

FOUR STEPS TO HANGING UP

Let's cut to the chase: many of you bought this book simply because you want nothing more than to rid yourselves of phone pests. Your compassion as a human being, however, may prevent you from simply hanging up. (This may also be a sign of codependency: by speaking to telemarketers, you are also acting as their "enabler.") Whatever the case, you need to know how to hang up quickly and effectively. Remember, to really help those on the other end of the line, we must discourage them from pursuing their current careers. Once you've correctly identified a telemarketer, use the four steps on the following pages to gain the confidence you need to free yourself from sales calls.

STEP 1. INTERRUPT THE TELEMARKETER.

This is perhaps the hardest step, most often because once a telemarketing pitch begins, it's hard for anyone to get a word in edgewise. It is, however, one of the most important aspects of phone solicitation deterrence: confronting telemarketing calls relies on actually speaking.

Beginners may wish to employ an "apologetic" approach: "I'm sorry, but I must hang up the phone now. This is very difficult for me. I'm going through a four-step program to help me learn to hang up on telemarketers. I don't blame you for the call or your unfortunate career choice—I hope you'll understand."

If you succeed with Step 1, proceed directly to Step 4. If not, go to Step 2.

Step 2. Walk Away.

If you can't bring yourself to interrupt a telemarketer, simply set the phone down and walk away. You can rest assured the caller will keep right on talking and never know you've gone.

Were you able to lay down the phone for at least one minute? Congratulations! You're making progress.

Now go back to Step 1 and try again to interrupt the caller, but this time speak before listening to the caller's voice—this way you give yourself the illusion that you're not actually interrupting.

If you couldn't set the phone down for at least one minute, proceed to Step 3.

STEP 3. PASS OFF THE CALL.

If even after Step 2 you cannot bring yourself to interrupt a telemarketer, try to get a housemate to do it for you.

Proceed with Step 2, but this time do not pick up the phone to interrupt the caller. Instead, yell, "Just a moment, please" loud enough so the caller can hear you. Next, tell your parent, spouse, or roommate—whoever's home at the time—that they have a call. If asked for the caller's identity, tell them "they didn't say."

Once your housemate picks up the phone and recognizes the caller is a telemarketer, they should be angry enough to hang up for you. (If they are not, buy them a copy of this book.)

Warning: While this step gets rid of the unwanted call, it also causes conflict in your interpersonal relationships and should be relied upon only if Steps 1 and 2 fail repeatedly. Be careful not to become dependent on house-mates to hang up for you, and keep practicing Steps 1 and 2 until you make progress. You will have achieved success when you reach Step 4 without hesitation.

STEP 4. HANG UP.

Once you have successfully accomplished Step 1 (whether directly or through Steps 2 and/or 3), you should have the confidence to hang up immediately. To do this, first locate the reset button and either depress it or set the receiver on top of it. The next time a telemarketer calls, you don't have to say anything, just hang up as soon as you have correctly identified a sales call.

CONGRATULATIONS!

You now know how to quickly and effectively rid your life of annoying telemarketers. The next two chapters focus on more complicated (and fun!) ways to shut down and turn the tables on telemarketers.

ANTI-TELEMARKETER MEDITATIONS

Learning to hang up is an ongoing process. To help you in your struggle, try using the "meditations" below—words to consider as you struggle with telemarketers:

I DIDN'T CALL

"I didn't place this call. I don't have to speak to this person, no matter how misguided he or she may be. It's ok for me to hang up. It's OK."

I DON'T WANT THIS

"I don't want a [product/service]. And I don't need it. There's no reason to continue speaking to this person, no matter how misguided he or she may be. It's ok for me to hang up. It's OK."

I WON'T ENABLE

"If I hang up, the telemarketer may become discouraged and seek other employment. That will help this person, no matter how misguided he or she may be. It's ok for me to hang up. It's OK."

CHAPTER 3

EFFICIENT ESCAPES

The new skills you learned in the first two chapters give you the upper hand in any confrontation with a telemarketer. You are now ready to employ what we call "efficient escapes" before you hang up. These "escapes" help make getting rid of telemarketers fun, at least for you. They rely on the two techniques you learned in Chapter 2: interrupting and hanging up. Think of these escapes as a duel with the telemarketer—only *you* always have the advantage: with your finger poised over the reset button, you hold the only loaded weapon. Feeling a little guilty over this unfair advantage? Don't. It's not your fault! Remember: they started it; they asked for it. They called you.

EFFICIENT ESCAPE 1

CONFUSE THE CALLER

If you're sure a telemarketer looms on the other end of your ringing phone, answer by saying: "Hi, I'd like to place an order to go," and continue by reading your favorite Chinese restaurant take-out menu. If the telemarketer doesn't do so on his or her own, HANG UP!

June Says: Oh, hello there! June here. Say, if you haven't already picked up one of them new caller ID units yet, go get one! They're great for spotting a telemarketer before you even pick up the receiver. They're just great!

Efficient Escape 2
PREY ON THEIR FEARS

Interrupt: "Thanks for calling—you've given me a chance to try out my new anti-telemarketer caller ID device. Your number is now programmed into the machine, so if you ever call here again, you will automatically be transferred to 1-900-BIG STUD, and I'm sure your supervisors will easily trace the charge back to you." HANG UP NOW!

EFFICIENT ESCAPE 3

CREATE A TECHNICAL DIFFICULTY

Interrupt by ignoring the telemarketer and saying, "Hello? Hello?" Click the reset button twice quickly, without hanging up, and repeat "Hello? Hello?" Follow by saying, "Well, whoever it was, they must have hung up." Then HANG UP! If they call back, repeat. If they call back more than three times, tell them you were just kidding, compliment them on their persistence, and HANG UP immediately!

Efficient Escape 4
Give Them a "Fair" Chance

If you are in the kitchen at the time of a call, set the oven timer for five seconds and interrupt the caller, explaining that he or she has until the buzzer sounds to deliver the pitch. Then hold the mouthpiece of the phone near the timer, press start, and yell, "Go!" When the timer rings, HANG UP!

Efficient Escape 5

REVERSE THE CHARGES

Next time a telemarketer calls, don't let them get their first sentence out before asking them for their billing address. When they ask "Why?" tell them: "Well, I'd be happy to talk with you, but I'm a Telemarketing Effectiveness Consultant and I charge for my evaluation of your performance. I need to know where to send the bill." Listen for the inevitable "click."

EFFICIENT ESCAPE 6

PRETEND YOU'RE AN ANSWERING MACHINE

If you've already made the mistake of saying, "Hello," pause for a second and interrupt the telemarketer with, "Sorry, but I can't come to the phone right now. If you could leave your name, number, and a brief message after the tone, I'll get back to you." Pressing one of the keypad keys usually passes for the electronic tone of an answering machine (the number "9" key works exceptionally well), but a brief, sharp whistle really annoys phone salespeople. When you hear the telemarketer begin their message, HANG UP!

Efficient Escape 7

Rehearse Your Vegas Act

Interrupt by breaking into song during the telemarketer's pitch. Don't stop until they hang up. If they remain on the line, soften your voice, creating a "fadeaway" effect and hang up after a few bars. Show tunes and anything by Ethel Merman tend to be the most effective, but nothing clears your phone line faster than your own rendition of Whitney Houston's "I Will Always Love You." Leave the hanging up to the telemarketer.

EFFICIENT ESCAPE 8

MENTION YOU ARE CURRENTLY BUSY

Interrupt: "Oh, very funny—I just gave birth to quadruplets, you know. Right now they're all crying: two need changing, one needs to be fed, and the other two managed to unscrew the incubator bulb. You think I have time to talk with you?" HANG UP NOW!

If nothing else, this escape's math problem should confuse the telemarketer enough to clear your line.

Efficient Escape 9

Appeal to Their Compassion

Interrupt: "Do you realize you called just as I was _____ ?" (Insert the appropriate activity from "Learn to Recognize the Ring" in Chapter One.) "What kind of human being are you? Where's your sensitivity? Your compassion?" Say this dramatically, as if you are on the verge of tears, then slam down the receiver (HANG UP!) as loudly as possible without damaging your phone.

Efficient Escape 10

EXPRESS JUBILANT DISBELIEF

Once the telemarketer indicates they have a "special offer" for you, interrupt with "For me? Really? Oh, this is great! After the bank foreclosed and I maxed out the credit cards, I thought I'd never get another chance! This is unbelievable! I don't need to be employed to order, do I?" When you hear the awkward pause on the other end of the line, HANG UP!

EFFICIENT ESCAPE 11

INDIRECTLY THREATEN THE CALLER

As soon as the telemarketer asks, "And how are you this evening?" answer: "Very frustrated! The damn phone has been ringing off the hook with people trying to sell me things. I swear, if one more telemarketer calls, somebody's going to pay for it! Now, what can I do for you?" When you hear the awkward pause on the other end of the line, HANG UP!

Efficient Escape 12

FEIGN EXCITEMENT

Interrupt: "Oh, I'm so glad that you called! I just finished a four-step program to learn how to hang up on telemarketers—and you're my first real call! Ready?" HANG UP NOW!

Efficient Escape 13

PROMISE TO CALL BACK

Another turn-the-tables escape like "Reverse the Charges," but this time ask the telemarketer for their home number. When they ask "Why?" tell them, "This way, I can wait until *you're* asleep and wake *you* up!" Again, listen for the inevitable "click."

Efficient Escape 14

Fake a "Call Waiting" Call

Similar to "Create a Technical Difficulty," this escape relies on your technical expertise with the Touch Tone™ phone. Once a phone solicitor breaks into their pitch, briefly hit the reset button (without hanging up!) to create a "click" and then apologize that you must take the incoming call, then click the reset button again without hanging up. At this point you have three options: 1) simply hang up and leave the telemarketer hanging; 2) after a moment, "click" back and explain the other call is an emergency and you must go; 3) pretend you haven't correctly switched lines: "Yeah, Bob, I've got this loser telemarketer on the other line. What kind of a slug does that for a living?"

EFFICIENT ESCAPE 15

900-FONE-FUN

Allow the telemarketer to begin the sales pitch. At the same time, start breathing heavily into the phone. When they pause to ask if you have any questions, breath a bit louder and say, "What are you wearing?" Your phone should be clear in a second. Works with same or mixed genders.

KNOW YOUR EQUIPMENT

The telemarketer is nothing without a telephone. In fact, statistics show that people who don't own phones are eighty percent less likely to receive a telemarketing call. To be better prepared to deal with phones salespeople, you must know how to use your telephone effectively. Once again, we have contacted an expert—Bob Schuck, formerly of United Telephone Monopolies, Inc.—to help us help you rid yourself of telemarketers. Learning to use specific features of the telephone will help you to perform several functions that will aid you in your fight against phone sales, including feigning line interference, pretending you're an answering machine, and most importantly, hanging up! Here's Bob's guide to using today's modern Touch Tone™ telephone:

▲ *Robert "Bob" Schuck, telecommunications specialist*
Independent Consultant License #42C-5WP94.01

THE TOUCH TONE TELEPHONE:
HERE'S THE BEAUTY OF THIS UNIT

"Your basic Touch Tone™ unit, though filled with remarkable capabilities, is the portal through which all your telemarketing encounters take place. Most Touch Tone™ phones include your base, your ringer, your receiver, your receiver cord, your outlet cord, your keypad, and your reset button. That's the beauty of this unit."

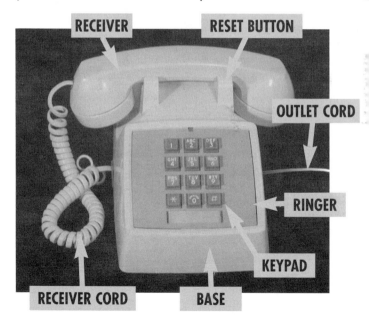

THE BASE

"The central unit of your telephone, the base, holds in place most of your electronic elements or 'guts' of the phone and acts as a central locality for connecting the various cords together. It's kind of like Grand Central Station if you will.

"It also includes your cradle, in which your receiver rests when not in use. Most bases also house your keypad and your reset button, although some of today's more streamlined models include those features as part of the receiver.

"The base unit is also key to phone safety. Should you decide to hurl your phone in frustration over a telemarketing call, make sure to include the base. I learned the hard way that if you just toss the receiver, the cord may cause it to snap back before you can get out of the way."

THE RINGER

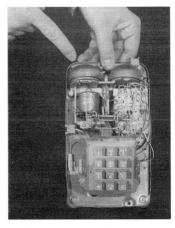

"Hidden deep within the telephone, the ringer (actually two bells) indicates an incoming call—this is your first sign that a telemarketer may be on the attack. I like to think of it as an early warning system. Of course, if you turn the ringer off, or, more permanently, rip the bells right out of your base unit, you can avoid telemarketing calls altogether."

EARPIECE

MOUTHPIECE

RECEIVER: EARPIECE & MOUTHPIECE

"Your receiver unit (shown here) is actually two pieces of equipment in one: your earpiece and your mouthpiece.

"Used for listening, the earpiece is the path through which a telemarketer attacks you. You can effectively block many attacks simply by keeping the earpiece away from your ear. The mouthpiece, on the other hand, is used by you to speak into the phone. This, then, is your weapon for counterattacking.

"In other words, the receiver—through which you both attack and are attacked—is really a double-edged sword in your battle against phone solicitors."

THE OUTLET CORD

"The outlet cord connects your base to your wall outlet, which connects your phone to the phone company, which connects you to the outside world and unfortunately, therefore, to telemarketers. In emergency phone sales situations, simply remove the cord from the back of your base unit (as shown above). I also suggest leaving it disconnected for at least an hour should the telemarketer attempt to reconnect. To more permanently thwart the telemarketer, clip the cord (as shown on right). Your basic #9 diagonal clippers should work just fine."

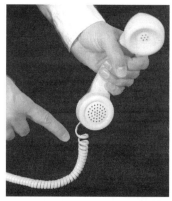

THE RECEIVER CORD

"Your coiled receiver cord connects the receiver to your base unit. The rapid unplugging and replugging of this cord can be used to falsify technical difficulties and thereby discourage your average phone solicitor."

June Says: Oh, hello there! June here. For a really clever guide to creating a technical difficulty, see "Create a Technical Difficulty" on page 22.

June Says: Oh, hello there! June here again. Some older phones, like my next-door neighbor Caroline's, use a "dial" instead of buttons. This is probably why they call it "dialing the phone." Dial phones come in handy when you reach those annoying answering systems that have replaced receptionists: since you can't press any buttons, the machine connects you with an actual person!"

▲ *Dial telephone circa 1965*

THE KEYPAD

"Buttons or 'keys' representing the numbers 0 to 9 are used primarily to place calls. Except for the '0,' the numbers are placed in easy-to-follow, numerical order. Most key pads also include the # (or 'pound') key and * (or 'star,' even though it's really an asterisk) key. Some phones use these special keys to operate features such as last number redial or speed dial. All twelve keys make their own unique 'beep' or 'tone' when touched, hence 'Touch Tone™.' In your battle against telemarketers, you won't be using the keypad to place any calls. You can, however, use the keys to help simulate an answering machine (see 'Pretend You're an Answering Machine' on page 25).

You may also wish to spend some time learning to play songs using the tones of the keypad keys. Nothing gets a telemarketer off your line faster than a high-pitched rendition of 'In-a gadda-da-vida.' For you beginners, try this combination of keystrokes to play 'Mary Had a Little Lamb': 6, 5, 4, 5, 6-6-6; 5-5-5; 6-6-6; 6, 5, 4, 5, 6-6-6; 6, 5-5, 6, 5, 4."

▲ *Play songs using your touch tone keys. Nothing clears your lines faster than a high-pitched rendition of "In-a-gadda-da-vida."*

THE RESET BUTTON

"In your fight against telemarketers, this is your most important weapon! Setting the receiver on top of the reset button—or simply depressing it—disconnects the incoming call. In other words, it *hangs up* the phone! When confronted with a sales call, never allow yourself to move out of reach of the reset button!"

CHAPTER 4

ELABORATE ENCOUNTERS

Now that you have learned to turn the tables—to become the hunter rather than the hunted—it's time to learn to play with your prey. This chapter outlines encounters you can enact in order to annoy telemarketers and ensure they never get their pitch off the ground. These are more involved than escapes and require patience and practice to effectively play them out. They still rely on the "interrupt and hang up" principle, but more often the phone solicitor will be the one disconnecting the call. A common element to many of these encounters is an old trick of the trade whereby you turn the approach of phone salespeople back on them—we are, of course, talking about talking: continuous, relentless, unyielding, inexorable, never-letting-up, nonstop talking.

Once you've mastered these, you will be ready to create your own. Soon you'll have an entire repertoire of telemarketer-deflating encounters to act out at your discretion—limited only by the extent of your imagination. You may, in fact, grow to look forward to your next encounter with a phone-toting salesperson.

$\mathcal{E}$LABORATE $\mathcal{E}$NCOUNTER #1

THE OLD CODGER / OLD CRONE

If the caller asks, "Is this the man [or woman] of the house?" tell them, "Just a minute, please," and pretend to hand the phone to "Dad" or "Grandpa" (or "Mom" or "Grandma") as the case may be. Then use your best "old codger" (or "old crone") voice and bombard the caller by repeating "Huh?" and "Speak up!" If they persist, go into a pointless, meandering, story that begins: "Why, back in my day we didn't …" Add drool-laden "slurp" noises for effect. The phone salesperson will soon give up.

ℰLABORATE ℰNCOUNTER #2

THE HOUSE FIRE

This routine works particularly well with telemarketers selling furnace, chimney, or ductwork cleaning. Once you have identified their service, break into tears and sob, "Is this some kind of a joke? My house burned down last night! We lost everything!" If they offer an apology, accept it graciously and hang up. If not, slam down the receiver. Either way you've left them with something to wonder about for a while.

ℰLABORATE ℰNCOUNTER #3

VEGGIEBABBLE

Based on the theory that you don't have to actually be psychotic to act crazy, this routine causes most telemarketers to question their career choice. When a telemarketer begins a pitch, arbitrarily begin inserting the names of vegetables as they try to speak. After the first or second "rutabaga" or "broccoli" they should respond by saying, "What?" Reply by naming another vegetable ("okra" and "Brussels sprouts" work particularly well). The salesperson will begin laughing uncomfortably and hang up. You win.

$\mathscr{E}$LABORATE $\mathscr{E}$NCOUNTER #4

VACUUM SALES

Is the telemarketer offering a "free" one-room carpet cleaning? Excellent! Don't pass this one up! Simply tell them to "Come right over! Right now! Because, believe it or not—What timing! This is great! You see, I'm fleeing—er, moving out of state—very, very soon. Everything is set to go, but this house is a rental and I'll never get the deposit back if I don't get this carpet cleaned. How soon could you guys get here? It will get blood stains out, won't it? How about identifiable fibers, like hair or that DNA stuff? You know, like in the O.J. trial? Say, you don't think he really did it, do you? You want to know my theory?" Again, run with this one as long as you can.

ELABORATE ENCOUNTER #5

WHAT DID I WIN?

As soon as you hear that familiar "This is so and so from such and such ..." cut the telemarketer short by saying, "I'm very busy right now. Please just tell me what I've won and when I should expect to receive it, OK? I'm in a big hurry." The speaker will try to continue his or her canned pitch. Interrupt again with a nonstop whirlwind of chatter: "I'll be in all next week, that will be a great time to deliver it. Maybe you should call first. And if for some reason I'm out, you can leave it at the neighbor's. They're always home. The Mr. works at home, you see, and Mrs. works nights at a... Well, that's beside the point. We shouldn't judge. At any rate, it won't be a problem to leave it on the front porch because we have a really good neighborhood watch program and...

Say, this prize won't affect my taxes too heavily, will it?" If the telemarketer is still on the line at this point, stop yourself in mid-sentence, feign panic, and say, "Oh, good lord! Ed McMahon's at the door!" and hang up.

$\mathcal{E}$LABORATE $\mathcal{E}$NCOUNTER #6

UNCLE EDGAR, DUCT TAPE PRO

Here's the ultimate furnace cleaning service retort. When telemarketers call with an offer to clean your furnace ductwork, ask in detail exactly how the company cleans ducts, volunteering your own ideas along the way: "How long does it take? You see, my daughter's fruit fly cultures are very fragile and the house needs to stay at exactly seventy-four degrees or they'll perish. How do you do it? I bet you set little robots loose in the ductwork with teeny mops soaked in pine cleaner so the whole house gets that just-cleaned north woods smell, right? You won't need to remove and replace the duct tape, will you? Boy, I hope not. My great-uncle Edgar built this house and taped the whole thing himself. Christmas wouldn't be the same without a trip downstairs to admire

Edgar's handiwork. He was quite an artisan, you know. Passed on about twenty years ago, I suppose—heck, it'll be twenty years to the day next Saturday. Maybe we should have a little get-together. I wonder what the family would say about a memorial…" Run with this one as long as you can—you'll eventually wear them out and will be well rewarded when you hear that victorious "click" of a terminated call.

ℰLABORATE ℰNCOUNTER #7

MAKING NEW FRIENDS

You can turn any telephone salesperson into an instant "lonely guy/gal companion" by enacting this simple scenario: "I'm so glad you called. I've been pretty lonely since my boy[girl]friend left me. Are you an Aries? You sound like an Aries. Say, if you wouldn't mind, I'd like to ask your opinion about something. Do you think your roommate has good reason to move out just because you like to bathe in Jell-o™ and it leaves a rubbery ring around the tub?" This works even better if you use a slow, monotonous voice. If the telemarketer persists, add "Sure, I'm interested. But only if you come over in person, OK? And maybe we could go see a movie or something. Or I could cook us dinner. You do like head cheese, don't you?" Your phone should be free shortly.

ℰLABORATE ℰNCOUNTER #8

HELLO, SPORTS FANS!

As soon as you identify a caller as a telemarketer, change the topic to sports: "Did you see the game last night?" Once you get started, keep going as long as you can and try to engage the telemarketer in a debate about coaching changes, quarterback controversies, pitching performances, etc., that involve his or her favorite team (say, for instance, the Green Bay Packers). If the caller works the sales pitch back into the conversation, say, "I'm sorry, I'd never buy anything from a Packers' fan. Cheesehead." And hang up.

ℰLABORATE ℰNCOUNTER #9

JUST WONDERING . . .

Midway through a telemarketer's opening remarks, interrupt as if your mind was wandering: "Did you ever think about what causes a hiccup?" If the telemarketer knows the answer, act amazed and ask another question immediately: "Wow, really? Then what makes a firefly's tail light up like that?" If the caller answers your second question, try the following questions until you come up with a stumper: "Why are fire engines red?" "What do you suppose would happen to England without the royal family?" "Where does the term 'by the skin of my teeth' come from?" "Why do they call dandelions 'dandelions'" "Is Jack Palance single?" "Why don't they just get rid of silent letters?" "Where does the white go when the snow melts?" "Why do you park on a driveway and drive on a parkway?" "Does water really swirl down the drain in a different direction south of the equator?"

If a phone solicitor knows the answers to all these questions, they have much bigger problems than earning commission. Tell them to get a life!

ELABORATE ENCOUNTER #10

MY DOG ATE THE PHONE CORD

Let the caller get about two sentences into the pitch while you establish the presence of a dog by employing your best fake muffled bark. Next, act distracted and apologize as you turn to yell at the fictitious pooch: (muffled bark) "No, King! Don't chew on that! Bad dog!" Add more muffled barking, then yell to someone in the background: "Criminy, honey, would you get the dog outta here? He's chewing on the phone cord agai—" At this point, hang up the phone or pull the outlet cord from the wall.

Elaborate Encounter #11

THE QUIET "PUT DOWN"

Respond with a patronizing "Yes, uh-huh, yes…" throughout the first few sentences of the telemarketer's pitch. Then, quietly set the phone down (without hanging up), leave the room, and take this opportunity to enjoy a nice, hot bubble bath, read a novel, or watch a rerun of "The Rockford Files." Your phone should be free within an hour or so.

ℰLABORATE ℰNCOUNTER #12

SIGN 'EM UP

Turn the sales call around as quickly as possible by pitching to the pitcher: "Say, how would you like to make an extra fifty to one hundred dollars a week by selling soap products right out of your own home? I've been selling a wonderful new cleaning solution to my friends and acquaintances: ZIPPYZUDS-480. You can sell it, too, and even sign up your friends to sell it and then you get a percentage of what they sell! Just give me your home address and phone number so I can send you a complete ZIPPYZUDS-480 brochure." They'll probably hang up, but some may actually give the information. Then simply say "Thank you. The brochure will be in the mail tomorrow" and hang up. Either way, your line's free.

$\mathscr{E}$LABORATE $\mathscr{E}$NCOUNTER #13

PRODUCT CRITICISM

If the phone solicitor is selling encyclopedias, deflect the call by saying, "Is this some kind of sick joke? Who put you up to this? It's well known in these parts that our youngest lost her life because of your encyclopedias! Why, if that shelf would've held under the weight of volumes M-Z, she'd still be with us today! A pox on you and your policy of using heavy, glossy paper and thick, hardbound covers!" Hang up.

$\mathscr{E}$LABORATE $\mathscr{E}$NCOUNTER #14

YOUR CHEATIN' HEART

The perfect encounter for when you receive a call from a telemarketer of the other sex. As soon as the phone salesperson says "Hello, I'm with—" cut them off quickly with a semi-whispered "Look, I thought I told you never to call me here." When they say "Excuse me?" go into your spiel: "Listen, my husband [wife] is in the other room! I told you it was over and I meant it! It's over! We're through! And I'm not giving in to any more of your blackmail, either! You can keep the Porsche, but I'm not paying for the apartment or any more Beverly Hills shopping sprees, you got it? Now, get out of my life!" Hang up.

This one's pretty effective, so we doubt they'll be calling you back. Come to think of it, this may work even better with a same-sex phone solicitor. Then again, maybe not. This whole preference thing is pretty complicated, and we don't want to offend anyone.

$\mathscr{E}$LABORATE $\mathscr{E}$NCOUNTER #15

"PUR-RAZE THE LO-WORD!"

After a few months manning phone lines, many telemarketers lose their faith in a number of things. Religion is no exception. Consequently, nothing scares them more than the possibility of connecting lines with an overzealous evangelist. You can take advantage of this fear by developing a Southern Baptist-influenced televangelist accent (a simple technique to achieve the proper tone is to add as many syllables as possible to mono- or bisyllabic words; for instance, the word "saved" should be spoken with no less than three syllables). Once you have the voice down, use the following dialogue to disarm a phone solicitor: "Son [Miss], with just five easy payments, I can guarantee you a seat at the right hand of our Savior." Before the telemarketer can reply, add, "Lord, your humble servants here at the Church of the Heavenly Cash Register pray for this child, so that he [she] may find his [her] way to You and by way of his [her] checkbook. Help him [her] see that the first step on the true path to heaven is a small down payment on salvation. Pur-raze the Lo-word!" If this doesn't immediately clear your lines, ask the caller to kneel and join you in prayer.

A NOTE TO READERS

You may have noticed that the our last elaborate encounter treats televangelists with the same disdain we have heretofore reserved for telemarketers. Coincidentally, both use the promise of a product or service (i.e. driveway resurfacing, carpet cleaning, eternal salvation, etc.) to persuade innocent people to part with large sums of money. One theory is that this absolutely tacky approach is somehow related to the "tele" prefix. The philosophical debate grows when you also bring long-distance *tele*phone companies and cable *tele*vision into the equation, and becomes ethically complicated when you consider *tele*thons that raise money for legitimate concerns. Once you mention *tele*pathy, however, it just gets plain silly.

CHAPTER 5

ALTERNATIVE EMPLOYMENT OPPORTUNITIES

If you haven't the heart to toy with telemarketers using the escapes or encounters of the previous two chapters, you may wish to kindly deflect their sales pitches by suggesting another, less offensive line of work. Remember, each phone solicitor you convince to find other employment means one less parasite phoning you, your friends, and your family. Telemarketers have developed skills that may help them secure positions in other industries. The step-by-step analysis of a typical sales call on the following pages will help us identify those skills.

BREAKDOWN OF A TYPICAL TELEMARKETING CALL

STEP 1

The telemarketer picks up the phone and determines if it is operating correctly and/or if he or she is connected with an open line by *listening for a signal*—a dial tone.

STEP 2

The telemarketer places a call in order to contact potential victims, or "customers," by *pushing buttons on the phone's keypad.*

STEP 3

The potential victim answers the call with the interrogative "Hello?" to which every telemarketer is trained to respond, originally enough, by also *saying "Hello."*

Step 4

The telemarketer initiates the sale by speaking to the victim, a person they have never met, using friendly, idle chatter—in other words, by *holding a conversation with a complete stranger.*

Step 5

The telemarketer dives into a prewritten sales pitch; basically, the telemarketer attempts to sell goods or services by *reading a script.*

Step 6

The telemarketer continues the pitch until the end, all the while *ignoring a customer's complaints.*

STEP 7

Even after the victim has insisted that he or she has no need of the telemarketer's product or service, the phone salesperson continues to push the product by *refusing to take "no" for an answer.*

STEP 8

After a while, the victim becomes fed up with the obnoxious caller and hangs up, so the telemarketer is left *facing continuous rejection*.

Now let's examine these telemarketing skills and discuss them as to their specific marketability in today's ever-shrinking workplace:

TRANSLATING TELEMARKETER SKILLS INTO OTHER PROFESSIONS

LISTENING FOR A SIGNAL

Psychologist. The best attribute of successful psychiatric counselors is the ability to listen. They have to pick out signals provided by a patient in order to identify his or her afflictions.

Of course, since we've established that many telemarketers already hold undergraduate psychology degrees but can't afford graduate school, suggesting this option may be cruel. Give it a try anyhow.

PUSHING BUTTONS.

Ten-Key Operator. The want ads are jam-packed with opportunities for "Ten-Key Operators." While we have no idea what these people do, they apparently operate—or "push"—ten keys—or 'buttons"—as a major part of their task.

However, since most telephones are equipped with twelve keys, telemarketers may, in fact, be overqualified for this position.

Thank you for shopping at ShopMart. Here's your cart.
Thank you for shopping at ShopMart. Here's your cart.
Thank you for shopping at ShopMart. Here's your cart.
Thank you for shopping at ShopMart. Here's your cart.
Thank you for shopping at ShopMart. Here's your cart.
Thank you for shopping at ShopMart. Here's your cart.
Thank you for shopping at ShopMart. Here's your cart.
Thank you for shopping at ShopMart. Here's your cart.

▲ *Knowing how to say "Hello" can open doors for former phone solicitors in the world of retail sales.*

Saying "Hello."

Giant Retail Store "Greeter." Since they already know how to use a phone, you would think that telemarketers would make natural receptionists. However, experienced phone solicitors often have trouble adjusting to *receiving* calls and find only limited happiness in transferring calls. At Wal-Mart and other major retailers, however, they can be retrained to think of shoving carts at incoming customers as their "sales pitch."

Holding a Conversation with a Complete Stranger.

Catholic Priest. Unfortunately, no one gets paid to ride the bus and irritate fellow passengers, so former telemarketers must find other ways to converse with those they don't know. People come to priests to confess their most vile acts—and, just like phone salespersons, priests in a confessional never have to face those they talk to.

Telemarketers have spent much of their time asking people to allow them to intrude on their free time. Imagine the irony as people come to them for forgiveness.

READING A SCRIPT.

Waiter/Waitress. Normally, one would associate reading a script with acting. However, since many telemarketers are already out-of-work actors struggling to pay off student loans for their ill-fated B.F.A. degrees, this idea may be as cruel as suggesting they attempt a career as a psychologist.

Many actors, however, have found careers in the food service industry—and hey, most restaurants offer employees a free meal on every shift!

IGNORING CUSTOMERS' COMPLAINTS

Customer Service Representative. Since you can't get paid for being a bad spouse or know-it-all parent, former phone solicitors could parlay their talent to ignore the pleadings of potential customers in the increasingly popular field of customer service.

With the ability to tune out complaints, customer bellyaching goes in one ear and out the other, assuring erstwhile telemarketers a stress-free work day.

▲ *The telemarketing talent of ignoring customer complaints can lead to lucrative, stress-free careers in the customer service field.*

Refusing to Take "No" for an Answer.

Janitor. Those that can't take "no" for an answer usually have few second dates—and probably not many first dates—leaving most ex-telemarketers with plenty of free evenings and weekends. Since you won't find a listing for "obnoxious jerk" in the want ads, suggest that one-time telemarketers try sweeping up after the rest of us. The custodial sciences have always held opportunities for those who can work nights and weekends.

Facing Continuous Rejection.

Writer. If they're not a Stephen King imitator, an attorney turned thriller author, an expert on human sexuality, or a former "close personal friend" of a celebrity who has found him- or herself facing significant jail time, telemarketers can forget about finding any legitimate way to publish their work.

Of course, they probably won't make any money in this new line of work, but at least they'll be emotionally prepared for the inevitable stacks of rejection letters.

▲ *Sure, they have no writing talent, but no one can face the constant onslaught of rejection like a former telemarketer.*

LEGITIMATE CONCERNS

Me again—Mrs. Millard America! Did you like our little book? I think it has some wonderful ideas, although I'm not sure I'd use them all myself, at least not when we have company.

I wanted to point out that not all telemarketers are trying to sell you something you don't need. Some actually represent worthy causes you may wish to support, like the Red Cross or the American Cancer Society or some other nice charity. You should take the time to find out about some of these organizations because they really need your help.

Be careful, though. Some charities that seem just fine on the surface turn out to be scams that stick most of the money they collect into their own pockets. These parasites are just panhandlers with a desk and a phone! Other scams prey on older folks and those who have trouble handling their finances, offering quick returns on investments. Always keep this old adage in mind: "If it sounds too good to be true, it probably is."*

If you are unsure of the caller's legitimacy, your best bet is to simply tell them, "I don't do business over the phone. Please send me your information." And don't do anything stupid like giving them your address! If they represent a legitimate concern and they have your phone number, they can get your address. Then you can settle back in front of the TV and get some serious shopping done!

* *The Federal Trade commission (FTC) has set specific guidelines for telemarketing. Under their guidelines, telemarketers must:*

- *Say that they're making sales calls.*

- *Identify the seller.*

- *Reveal the nature of the goods or services being offered.*

- *If the call is about a prize promotion, say that no purchase or payment is necessary to win. (this must be disclosed before or in conjunction with the description of the prize.)*

Telemarketers cannot:

- *Call a consumer who has asked the company to not call again.*

- *Call a consumer before 8 a.m. or after 9 p.m.*
- *Withdraw money from a consumer's bank account without express, verifiable authorization.*
- *Make a false statement of any kind to induce payment, regardless of the payment method.*
- *Seek payment until after credit repair services, recovery-room service, or advance fee loan/credit services have been rendered.*

If you encounter a telemarketer who does not follow these guidelines, get the company's name and address, and note the date and time at which you were contacted. Then register a complaint with the Federal Trade Commission, 6th and Pennsylvania Avenue N.W., Washington, DC 20580.

To report telemarketing fraud, call the National Fraud Information Center at 800-876-7060 or your state attorney general's office.

You can also reduce the number of calls from national telemarketing firms by writing Telephone Preference Service at P.O. Box 9014, Farmingdale, New York 11735-9014.

THESE BAD DOG APPAREL ITEMS SHOW YOU HAVE:
A. A great sense of humor
B. Great taste in humor books
C. A limited wardrobe budget
D. A limited wardrobe
E. All of the above

NUKE THE TELEMARKETERS *tee #TEL001*

100% MONEY-BACK QUALITY GUARANTEE

Robert
BOB
SCHUCK
"That's the beauty of this unit."

JUST HANG UP

BACK DESIGN

★FREE★
BOB SCHUCK FAN CLUB membership card with every Bob Schuck shirt

BOB SCHUCK *tee #TEL002*

COOL BAD DOG STUFF

Your life won't be complete without these quality BAD DOG items.*

*Completeness of individual lives may vary

Back of mug says:

I ❤ MY BAD DOG

BAD DOG MUG *#BD003*

SAVE HUGE BUCKS ON A LITTER OF FOUR BAD DOG MUGS *#BD004*

Cap Back Design

BAD DOG PRESS

BAD DOG CAP *#BD002*

BAD DOG LOGO *Sweat #BD001S*
BAD DOG LOGO *T-Shirt #BD001T*

ORDERING INFORMATION

You can order by mail* or phone.
Fill out this handy order form prior
to calling so you don't forget anything.

_____	Nuke the Telemarketers T-Shirt *(TEL001)*	. . . .$17.95
_____	Bob Schuck T-Shirt *(TEL002)*	. . . .$17.95

_____	Bad Dog Logo T-Shirt *(BD001T)*	. . . .$17.95
_____	Bad Dog Logo Sweat *(BD001S)*	. . . .$27.95
_____	Bad Dog Embroidered Cap *(BD002)*	. . . .$19.95
_____	Bad Dog Mug *(BD003)*	. . . .$8.95
_____	Set of 4 Bad Dog Mugs *(BD004)*	. . . .$25.00

XXL size t-shirts and sweats add $1.50
MN residents add 6.5% tax on non-apparel items
Allow two to three weeks for delivery
Shipping/handling charges: $5.00

Pick One:
☐ Free Button
☐ Free Bumper Sticker

FREE BUTTON OR BUMPER STICKER WITH EVERY ORDER

Sub Total Items $	_____
Tax $	_____
Shipping Charges $	$5.00
Total $	_____

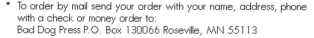

BAD DOG TOLL-FREE ORDER LINE
1-800-270-5863
`VISA` `MasterCard`

* To order by mail send your order with your name, address, phone
with a check or money order to:
Bad Dog Press P.O. Box 130066 Roseville, MN 55113

DO YOUR BAD DOG SHOPPING ON-LINE:
http://www.octane.com

BITE INTO THESE OTHER

BOOKS

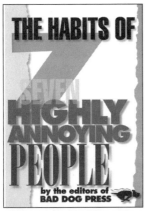

You know the type: they encourage mimes; they pass you on the highway and then drive too slow; they talk during movies; too often, they're your relatives. They're highly annoying people, and they play a much larger role in your life than do the highly effective.

Bad Dog's *The Habits of Seven Highly Annoying People* explores and exploits some of the most vexatious folks you'll ever meet. Great to give as an anonymous gift to people you find particularly annoying!

Has your soul had enough chicken soup to make you gag? The souls at Bad Dog Press sure have, so to cleanse America's palate they're offering *Rubber Chickens for the Soul,* a parody of the popular, inspiration-laden *Chicken Soup for the Soul* books.

While the stories in Rubber Chickens may not exactly open the heart and rekindle the spirit like those in the "Chicken Soup" books, they'll at the very least rekindle your heartburn.

Perhaps you've never made the mistake of showing up for an interview wearing a tie that requires batteries or listing "donating plasma" under your résumé's employment experience section. Well, the authors of *Who Packed Your Parachute?* have, and they hope their book can help others to avoid making similar errors. Here is the complete guide to what NOT to do during a job search.

Who Packed Your Parachute is the perfect book for graduates, adult children living with their parents, and anyone else on a job search.

A WHOLE NEW BREED OF HUMOR BOOKS!

Like our namesakes, we at Bad Dog Press aren't afraid to dig in the trash, chew the furniture, or take off dragging the leash—but we do so with tasteful, funny books that will have you laughing all the way home from the bookstore.

As you read this, the folks at Bad Dog are busy preparing other books that you'll love! Watch your bookstore humor section for our latest releases.

HAVE A PEEK AT OUR FUTURE BOOKS!

Visit the BAD DOG Humor On-Line Web page to preview upcoming books, participate in fun contests, join in funny forums, and find out how you can contribute to future Bad Dog books.
http://www.octane.com